I Spy

Anne Montgomery

I spy something blue.

It goes here.

I see it is a **square**.

It goes here, too.

I spy something red.

It goes here.

I see it is a **circle**.

It goes here, too.

I spy something green.

It goes here.

I see it is a **triangle**.

It goes here, too.

I spy something new.

It goes here.

I see it is art.

It goes here, too.

Let's Do Science!

How can you group things?
Try this!

What to Get

- ❑ 20 small items, such as pebbles, coins, or beans

What to Do

1. How are the items the same? How are they different?

2. Group the items by size. How many sizes do you see? Group the items by color. How many colors do you see?

3. How many ways can you group the items?

Glossary

circle — ●

square — ■

triangle — ▲

Index

art, 16

blue, 2

circle, 8

green, 10

red, 6

square, 4

triangle, 12

Your Turn!

How many ways can you group the things above?

Consultants

Sally Creel, Ed.D.
Curriculum Consultant

Leann Iacuone, M.A.T., NBCT, ATC
Riverside Unified School District

Jill Tobin
California Teacher of the Year
Semi-Finalist
Burbank Unified School District

Publishing Credits
Conni Medina, M.A.Ed., *Managing Editor*
Lee Aucoin, *Creative Director*
Diana Kenney, M.A.Ed., NBCT, *Senior Editor*
Lynette Tanner, *Editor*
Lexa Hoang, *Designer*
Hillary Dunlap, *Photo Editor*
Rachelle Cracchiolo, M.S.Ed., *Publisher*

Image Credits: Cover & pp.1–17, 20–21, p.24 Hillary Dunlap; pp.18–19 (illustrations) J.J. Rudisill; all other images from Shutterstock.

Library of Congress Cataloging-in-Publication Data

Montgomery, Anne (Anne Diana), author.
 I spy / Anne Montgomery.
   pages cm
   Summary: "It is time to learn about sorting things."—Provided by publisher.
   Audience: K to grade 3.
   Includes index.
   ISBN 978-1-4807-4525-4 (pbk.) —
   ISBN 978-1-4807-5134-7 (ebook)
 1. Science--Methodology—Juvenile literature.
 2. Classification--Juvenile literature. I. Title.
   Q175.2.M64 2015
   507—dc23
                                            2014008925

Teacher Created Materials

5301 Oceanus Drive
Huntington Beach, CA 92649-1030
http://www.tcmpub.com

ISBN 978-1-4807-4525-4
© 2015 Teacher Created Materials, Inc.